D1085284

EXPLORING
ANCIENT EGYPT

by Laura K. Murray

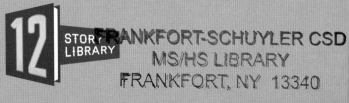

www.12StoryLibrary.com

12-Story Library is an imprint of Bookstaves and Press Room Editions

Produced for 12-Story Library by Red Line Editorial

Photographs ©: Pius Lee/Shutterstock Images, cover, 1; Schwabenblitz/Shutterstock Images, 4; erichon/Shutterstock Images, 5; Vladimir Korostyshevskiy/Shutterstock Images, 6, 29; Everett Historical/Shutterstock Images, 7, 8–9, 10, 11, 14, 25; Stephanie Pilick/picture-alliance/dpa/AP Images, 8, 28; Nasser Nasser/AP Images, 12; NYU Excavations at Amheida Staff (photographer), "Paintings from the tomb of Petosiris at Muzawaka (XIII)," Ancient World Image Bank (New York: Institute for the Study of the Ancient World, 2009-) <https://www.flickr.com/photos/isawnyu/>, used under terms of a Creative Commons Attribution license, 13; topolov/Shutterstock Images, 15; Guy Bell/Rex Features/AP Images, 17; McKay Savage CC2.0, 18; Daniel Kalker/picture-alliance/dpa/AP Images, 19; Sompol/Shutterstock Images, 20; Nicku/Shutterstock Images, 20–21; Jae C. Hong/AP Images, 22; Paolo Gallo/Shutterstock Images, 23; tunart/iStockphoto, 24; tepic/iStockphoto, 26

Content Consultant: Jennifer R. Houser Wegner, Adjunct Assistant Professor of Near Eastern Languages & Civilizations (Egyptology), University of Pennsylvania School of Arts & Sciences

Library of Congress Cataloging-in-Publication Data
Names: Murray, Laura K., 1989- author.
Title: Exploring Ancient Egypt / by Laura K. Murray.
Other titles: Exploring ancient civilizations (12 Story Library (Firm))
Description: Mankato, MN : 12 Story Library, 2018. | Series: Exploring
    ancient civilizations
Identifiers: LCCN 2016047643 (print) | LCCN 2016051801 (ebook) | ISBN
    9781632354624 (hardcover : alk. paper) | ISBN 9781632355270 (pbk. : alk.
    paper) | ISBN 9781621435792 (hosted e-book)
Subjects: LCSH: Egypt--Civilization--Juvenile literature.
Classification: LCC DT61 .M79 2018 (print) | LCC DT61 (ebook) | DDC 932--dc23
LC record available at https://lccn.loc.gov/2016047643

Printed in the United States of America
022017

Access free, up-to-date content on this topic plus a full digital version of this book. Scan the QR code on page 31 or use your school's login at 12StoryLibrary.com.

Table of Contents

Ancient Egyptian Civilization Lasted 3,000 Years

For more than 3,000 years, ancient Egyptians created a rich culture. They built pyramids, sculptures, and boats. They buried mummies. They raised families and played games. They farmed the land and used mathematics to tell time.

Ancient Egypt was located in northeastern Africa. The civilization existed alongside the Nile River. People first settled by the river to farm. These settlements grew bigger over time. The Nile flows from south to north, and its features created two areas. Southern Egypt was known as Upper Egypt. This was the Nile Valley. Northern Egypt was called Lower Egypt. This was the Nile Delta.

During its long history, Ancient Egypt had many rulers. The kings were known as pharaohs. Some rulers were women, but there weren't many of them. The pharaohs were part of groups or family lines called dynasties. The First Dynasty began around 3150 BCE. At this time, King Narmer united Egypt into one nation-state. Upper Egypt had more cities. Lower Egypt was more rural. Researchers aren't sure, but King Narmer probably conquered Lower Egypt to help supply food for the cities in Upper Egypt. He founded

The Nile Delta flows into the Mediterranean Sea.

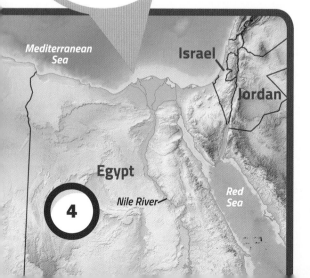

Mediterranean Sea

Israel

Jordan

Egypt

Nile River

Red Sea

4

The Nile River provides water for Egyptians today.

the city of Memphis as the capital. Memphis was located a few miles south of present-day Cairo.

During the rest of the dynasties, the empire grew bigger.

The ancient Egyptians started living in more cities. They built a large step pyramid. They created complex religious practices. By the time the Third Dynasty ended in approximately 2613 BCE, a unified Egyptian culture existed.

4,132
Length, in miles (6,650 km), of the Nile River.

- Ancient Egypt was located in northeastern Africa.
- The Nile River helped create Upper and Lower Egypt.
- Ancient Egyptian rulers were part of dynasties.
- Ancient Egyptian history includes the Old, Middle, and New Kingdoms.
- Memphis was the first capital city of ancient Egypt.

KINGDOMS OF EGYPT

Today, ancient Egypt is divided into time periods called kingdoms. But researchers do not agree on the exact years of each period. The Old Kingdom took place from around 2686 to 2125 BCE. The Middle Kingdom lasted from approximately 2055 to 1650 BCE. The New Kingdom took place around 1550 to 1069 BCE.

5

Egyptians Built Pyramids of Stone

Ancient Egyptians were master builders. The early kings built mastabas as tombs. These were rectangular structures made of mud-brick. They had a chapel aboveground and a burial chamber belowground. In approximately 2670 BCE, King Djoser wanted something different. His architect, Imhotep, designed a building that resembled six smaller mastabas stacked on top of one another. This became the first step pyramid.

Advances in architecture continued during the Old Kingdom. Later kings built pyramids of stone with smooth sides. These are known as true pyramids. Pyramids were part of complexes that included tombs, temples, smaller pyramids, and other buildings. The best known pyramid complexes are at the Giza Plateau. This place is home to the Great Pyramid of King Khufu. The Great Pyramid was built in approximately 2550 BCE. It took close to 20 years to finish being built. It rises 481 feet (147 m) from the sandy plain.

People today are still trying to understand how the Egyptians built the amazing pyramids. Many think workers cut and flooded ditches to level the land. Then they made

The step pyramid of King Djoser

2.3 million
Blocks of limestone in the Great Pyramid.

- Ancient Egyptians built palaces, temples, and monuments.
- Pyramids were used as burial places for kings.
- King Djoser made the first step pyramid.
- Pyramid builders came from all parts of society.
- People are still trying to understand how the pyramids were made.

BUILDING A PYRAMID

Large pyramids needed thousands of workers. These workers were not slaves. Instead, they came from different parts of society. Many worked for only part of the year. They were forced to work on building projects as a form of tax. The government gave them housing and food.

paths for dragging giant blocks. They likely used sleds, ramps, levers, and pulleys to get the stones in place.

They used copper tools for cutting and drilling. They used the stars to make everything align.

Egyptians also built great monuments, such as the Great Sphinx of Giza. Scientists aren't sure exactly when the sphinx was created. But most think it was built in approximately 2500 BCE. This enormous sculpture with the body of a lion and the head of a king is still standing.

A tourist in 1880 stands atop the Great Sphinx.

The King Ruled Over All

Everyone knew their place in Ancient Egyptian society. Ruling over everyone was the all-powerful king.

He was seen as the god Horus, son of Osiris. He was the head of government, military, and trade. He was also the high priest. There were a few women rulers, too. The female pharaoh Hatshepsut ruled for nearly 15 years during the New Kingdom.

Below the king were close advisers and government officials. Nobles and high priests came next. Other mid-level people included doctors, engineers, priests and priestesses, and scribes. Scribes were skilled writers. They recorded all sorts of information. This was very

Queen Nefertiti, who ruled alongside King Akhenaten

170

Approximate number of pharaohs of ancient Egypt.

- Everyone had their place in society.
- The Egyptian king ruled over everyone.
- Most ancient Egyptians made up the lower classes.
- Peasants were fishers and farmers.

Ramses II ruled over Egypt for 66 years.

important since most ancient Egyptians could not read or write.

Most Egyptians were part of the lower classes. There were soldiers, merchants, and builders. Artists and craftspeople made clothing, furniture, pottery, and more. At the bottom of society was the peasant class. They were fishers and farmers. They worked the land that others owned. Ancient Egypt also had some slaves who were usually prisoners of war. After the Old Kingdom, some in the lower classes gained more power. But the life of peasants did not change much.

Religion Explained
How the World Works

Ancient Egyptian civilization had many gods and goddesses. Horus was an important god of the sky and of kings. Sometimes Horus is shown as a falcon. He was the son of Osiris and Isis. Osiris was the god of the dead. After Osiris was murdered, his wife, Isis, brought him back to life. Egyptians saw Isis as the pharaoh's link between life and death. As the mother of Horus, Isis was especially important to Egyptian queens.

Egyptians worshipped a small group of local gods. They kept the statue of their god inside a temple.

There they offered the god food, drink, and clothing. They performed special rituals.

Certain gods were more powerful at different times in history. In the New Kingdom, the King of the Gods was Amen-Re. But when King Akhenaten took over in 1352 BCE, things changed. Like his father, he insisted that everyone should worship the sun god Aten instead of Amen-Re. He also said only Aten should be

Osiris (right) was often painted in tombs.

A rabbit-eared cat was associated with the sun god Ra.

worshipped, not any of the other gods and goddesses.

Stories about the gods helped explain why the sun rose or the Nile flooded. In one myth, the god Khnum formed humans on a potter's wheel.

The idea of ma'at was an important piece of Egyptian religion. To the Egyptians, having ma'at was to have harmony, truth, and order. The opposite of ma'at was chaos. Without ma'at, Egyptians believed bad things would happen, such as crops failing.

Everyone was responsible for keeping ma'at. The king communicated with the gods and oversaw rituals. Other Egyptians made offerings to the gods. They had to honor the king and lead good lives. They believed all of this would lead to life after death.

2

Eyes of Horus, where one was the sun and one was the moon.

- Ancient Egyptians had many gods and goddesses.
- They offered the gods food, drink, and clothing.
- Myths about the gods and goddesses helped explain the world.
- Everyone was responsible for keeping ma'at.

THINK ABOUT IT

Draw a picture of what you think an ancient Egyptian god or goddess looked like. Now visit the library or go online to see some examples. How does your picture compare?

Mummies Needed Food

Ancient Egyptians believed that life would continue after death. They believed they needed to preserve dead bodies for their souls to reach the afterlife. Bodies were mummified, or dried so they did not decay. The first mummies were probably accidents caused by the hot and dry desert sand. Egyptians began to purposely create mummies in approximately 2600 BCE. Kings and nobles were carefully mummified and buried in expensive tombs.

Poorer people used less expensive types of mummification.

There were special steps to mummification. First priests removed most of the organs from inside the body. They pulled the brain out through the nostrils. They left the heart in place. Next they packed the body with a salt called natron. This removed all moisture from the body. Once the body was dry, priests wrapped it in strips of linen. They coated each layer of linen with resin, a sticky substance

Mummy of Queen Tiye, the grandmother of Pharaoh Tutankhamen

from trees. They added amulets for good luck and protection.

Paintings from the tomb of a high priest

Meanwhile, workers and artists prepared the tomb. They added paintings, furniture, written prayers, and other items the person might need. The mummy also needed food and drink for the long, difficult journey to the afterlife. Lists or pictures of food worked, too.

Priests held a funeral at the mummy's tomb. Then the mummy was put inside his or her coffin. The tomb was sealed.

After death, Egyptians believed the person would be judged by the gods. Their heart would be weighed against a feather. The feather represented ma'at. If the heart was lighter than the feather, the person could enter the afterlife.

70
Days needed for mummification.

- Ancient Egyptians believed there was life after death.
- Dead bodies were mummified to help their souls reach the afterlife.
- Priests performed mummifications.
- A mummy's tomb held paintings, writings, food, drink, and more.

THREE IMPORTANT PARTS

Ancient Egyptians believed there were three parts to the soul. One was the *ka*. This was the person's life force and looked just like them. It needed food, drink, and clothing. The *ba* was the person's personality. It looked like a bird. It could fly from the tomb and return. The *akh* was the form that moved through the afterlife.

The Nile Flooded Each Year

Most of Egypt is a desert. People began to settle along the banks of the Nile River because it offered water and food. This long river was central to ancient Egyptian life. It gave water for drinking and washing. It helped people travel, communicate, and trade. It also nourished crops.

Farming was based on the annual flooding of the Nile River. The Nile began to rise in June and flooded in August. By October, the waters left behind large amounts of silt. This made the soil rich for growing crops. Farmers used plows, hoes, baskets, scoops, and other basic tools. Sometimes they used cattle to pull plows.

Egyptians used baskets when harvesting wheat.

Fig trees still grow all over Africa.

Ancient Egypt's main crops were barley and emmer wheat. These grains were made into bread and beer, the main food and drink. The Egyptians planted figs, grapes, beets, onions, and beans along the Nile. Farmers kept cattle, goats, and pigs. Egyptians would also catch wild birds that flocked to the Nile. They caught perch and catfish in the river's waters.

Without much water elsewhere, the Egyptians had to make the most of the Nile's flood each summer. Egyptians tried to control where the water went to make more farmland. They built dykes and raised walls. Farmers used tools to create channels for irrigation.

75

Percentage of Ancient Egyptian population who were farmers.

- Farming was based on the annual flooding of the Nile River.
- The Egyptians' main crops were barley and emmer wheat.
- Tools helped Egyptians control the flow of floodwaters.

15

Ancient Egyptians Had Specific Roles in Home Life

In many ways, home life for ancient Egyptians was just like other civilizations at the time. Men were expected to work and provide for their families. Women ran the household and cared for the children. Women usually did not work outside of the home. A woman's status in society was largely determined by who her father was and who her husband was.

But there were some ways Egyptian culture was very different. Women of ancient Egypt had the same legal rights as men. Wives were allowed to represent their husbands in business matters. They could buy property, bring lawsuits, and sign contracts. Egyptian women could also get divorced and remarry.

Children had toys and sometimes played games. But they had to help their parents, too. Girls helped in the house or helped care for younger siblings. A boy was expected to stay close to his father and learn how to do his job.

The sons of scribes and nobles went to school. They learned subjects

33

Average length of life for male peasants in ancient Egypt.

- Fathers earned a living.
- Mothers raised the children and ran the house.
- Women had the same legal rights as men.
- Girls were expected to help in the home, and boys were expected to help their fathers.

such as spelling, religion, and math. Some nobles hired tutors for their children. Most young girls did not go to school. But some still learned how to read and write. Children of the peasant class did not go to school.

Ancient Egyptian girls were usually around 14 years old when they got married. Boys were 16 to 20 years old. Most Egyptians married a person within their own class. They likely did not have a marriage ceremony. The couple lived in a home together or with their parents. Then they began a family of their own.

Ancient Egyptian children had some toys like this wooden horse.

The Egyptians Wrote in Hieroglyphs

The ancient Egyptian language was first used more than 5,000 years ago. It is one of the oldest recorded languages we know about. Ancient Egyptians wrote using hieroglyphs. These pictures or signs were written with ink or carved into stone. They were used for royal, religious, or historical writings. A hieroglyphic text could be written in horizontal lines or vertical columns. It could be written left-to-right or right-to-left. Hieroglyphic writing was used for more than 3,500 years. During that time, hieroglyphs changed very little. Another type of writing was demotic. It was a cursive writing used for letters and other everyday documents.

Scribes wrote on papyrus, wood, leather, or stone. The Egyptians believed that writing a symbol gave it life. It would live on as long as the writing remained.

Ancient Egyptians left records about everyday life in their art. The artists used pens made of reeds or brushes made of plant fibers. They made

Scribes wrote out a collection of spells for the afterlife, now called *The Egyptian Book of the Dead.*

Tourists can see the Rosetta Stone at the British Museum.

colors by mixing things such as iron ore, crushed stones, charcoal, and chalk. They decorated the walls of temples and tombs. They painted scenes of life on Earth and the afterlife. They showed people working, fighting, and dancing. They left instructions for the dead.

Other types of art included pottery, jewelry, and sculptures. Egyptian sculptors made carvings from stone, wood, and metals. They made carvings on tomb walls, too.

THE ROSETTA STONE

For hundreds of years, researchers could not understand the ancient Egyptian language. Then in 1799, an officer in the French army discovered a 1,500-pound (680 kg) black stone in Rosetta, Egypt. The stone was carved with the same text in three different scripts: hieroglyphs, an Egyptian cursive script called demotic, and ancient Greek. Scholars used the ancient Greek to translate the hieroglyphs. The Rosetta Stone became the key to understanding the ancient Egyptian language.

The Egyptians Were Skilled at Math

Egyptians used arithmetic and geometry. Math helped the Egyptians measure fields and plan pyramids. Some Egyptian math texts were written on papyrus or wooden tablets. They explained how to do math in everyday life. Others were sample math problems.

Ancient Egyptians also studied the moon and stars. They used them to make two calendars. One calendar was used by priests. A new year started when the star Sirius could be seen just before dawn in midsummer. But the calendar followed the moon's cycle. It had 12 months that were usually 28 or 29 days long. Sometimes a 13th month had to be added to stay on track with Sirius.

In approximately 3000 BCE, Egyptians who weren't priests decided to use a simpler calendar for everyday life. This one did not vary. It was always 365 days long. It did not depend on the

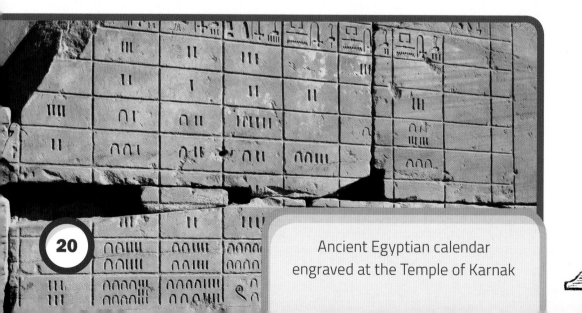

Ancient Egyptian calendar engraved at the Temple of Karnak

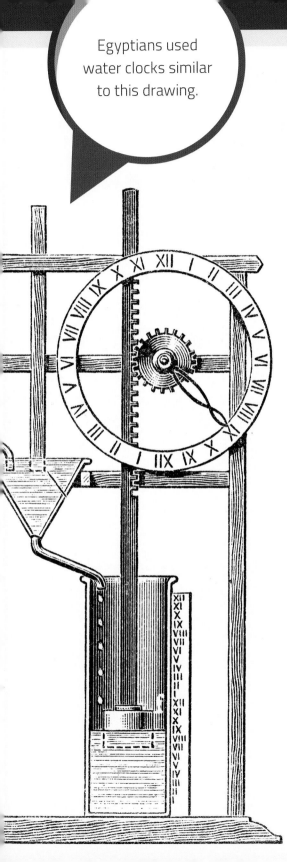

Egyptians used water clocks similar to this drawing.

1700 BCE

Approximate date the Moscow Papyrus was written, one of Egypt's oldest mathematical texts.

- Ancient Egyptians used arithmetic and geometry.
- One calendar followed the moon and was used by priests.
- One calendar was for everyday life and used math only.
- Sundials and water clocks were used to tell time.

moon or the sun. This was very unusual at the time. Most calendars from other ancient civilizations did not rely on math alone.

Egyptians also had different ways to tell time. Sundials used the movement of shadows. Water clocks used a steady drip of water to track the hours in a day. Water clocks could be used at night as well as in the day.

21

10

Ancient Egyptians Wore Wigs and Played Games

The Ancient Egyptians cared a lot about fashion. Women wore long linen dresses. Men of all classes wore kilts, which were pieces of linen wrapped around their hips. They added cloaks in winter. They carried staffs that showed their social class. During the New Kingdom, Egyptians began wearing new types of fashions. They wore long linen robes or shirts that tied at the neck.

People decorated their outfits with beads, ribbons, and trimmings. Both men and women wore jewelry of shells, stones, and animal teeth or bones. Some went barefoot. Others wore sandals. They wore wigs made of human hair or plant fibers.

Ancient Egyptians wore perfume made of oils, herbs, flowers, and fruits. Both men and women wore makeup, such as black eye paint called kohl. This wasn't just for beauty. The eye makeup protected against the bright sun and eye infections.

Egyptian women were proud of their wigs.

Senet is one of the oldest known board games.

Ancient Egyptians enjoyed playing games and sports. People played board games such as senet. In this game, players used sticks as dice to try to get their set of game pieces to the other side of the board first. Children played ball, tug-of-war, and other games. The Egyptians held contests to show their athletic skills. They wrestled, caught birds, and shot bows and arrows.

People swam, boated, and hunted crocodiles on the Nile. They also liked to sing and dance. They played instruments, such as flutes, drums, harps, and tambourines.

30
Number of squares on a senet board.

- Women and men wore clothing made of linen.
- Egyptians added beads, ribbons, trimmings, and jewelry to their outfits.
- Both men and women wore makeup.
- Ancient Egyptians played board games such as senet.
- Egyptians enjoyed music and athletic activities.

THINK ABOUT IT

What types of games do children play today? How do you think ancient Egyptian children's games were similar? How might they be different?

The Ancient Egyptian Empire Was Destroyed Slowly

The ancient Egyptian empire was slowly destroyed over a long period of time. As early as 1070 BCE, there were signs of trouble. At that time, Egypt was split in two. Lower Egypt was still ruled by the pharaoh. But Upper Egypt was ruled by a high priest. This lack of unity weakened the empire and paved the way for numerous invasions. In 728 BCE, the Nubians took over Egypt. Next the Assyrians had control, followed by the Persians. Throughout these conquests, though, Egyptian culture and religion survived.

Things changed in 332 BCE, when Alexander the Great took power. After Alexander's death, Egypt was controlled by Macedonian Greeks. The government used the Greek language instead of Egyptian. Macedonian Greeks continued to rule as pharaohs until 30 BCE. Cleopatra VII became the last pharaoh until she was defeated by the Romans.

Alexander the Great

This sculpture of Cleopatra and her son survived destruction.

Egypt was absorbed into the much larger Roman Empire. Over time, Egyptian culture and religion started to fade. As Christianity grew popular with Romans, it spread to Egypt. Christian churches became more and more powerful. Since Egyptian gods and goddesses appeared in hieroglyphs, the Christians wanted to replace the language with a new alphabet. The last known carving of hieroglyphs was made in 394 CE. Temples made to worship Egyptian gods and goddesses were all closed by 553 CE.

70
Number of cities that Alexander the Great founded while creating the Macedonian empire.

CLEOPATRA VII

Cleopatra VII is one of the most popular figures from ancient Egypt. She shows up in books, plays, and movies. Often she is depicted as being very beautiful. But researchers aren't exactly sure what she looked like. After she was defeated in 30 BCE, the Roman Octavian ordered most images of Cleopatra destroyed.

- Ancient Egyptian civilization had a long, slow decline.
- Alexander the Great invaded in 332 BCE.
- Cleopatra VII was the last pharaoh of ancient Egypt.
- Christianity played a big part in burying Egyptian religion and hieroglyphs.

Ancient Egyptian Mysteries Remain

For many years, the culture of ancient Egypt was largely forgotten. But things began to change in the Renaissance period in Europe during the 1500s and 1600s. People started to become interested in ancient civilizations. In 1798, the French general Napoleon invaded Egypt. His researchers discovered many Egyptian treasures. This led to renewed interest in Egyptian culture. It also led to the start of Egyptology, the study of ancient Egypt.

Egyptology got a huge boost in 1922 when the tomb of King Tutankhamun was discovered. King Tut's burial site was mostly untouched by grave robbers. Inside were jewelry, furniture, weapons, golden chariots, flowers, animal statues, and other treasures. King Tut's mummy rested inside a solid gold coffin. This discovery gave people a window into ancient Egypt as it truly existed.

King Tut's burial mask

THE DEATH OF KING TUT

King Tut is often called "the boy-king." He was just 9 or 10 years old when he became pharaoh. He was only 19 when he died. Researchers still aren't sure why King Tut died so young. Some think he was murdered, since the next pharaoh married King Tut's wife. Others say he died from an accident, because he broke his leg a few days before he died.

63

Number of tombs found in the Valley of the Kings so far.

- Napoleon's researchers discovered many Egyptian treasures.
- The study of ancient Egypt is called Egyptology.
- The discovery of King Tut's tomb increased interest in ancient Egypt.
- Ancient Egypt continues to fascinate people, since many mysteries remain.

Since then, archaeologists have combed through Egypt, looking to unearth more clues about the ancient civilization. They have uncovered tombs, monuments, hieroglyphs, ancient objects, and mummies. Many artifacts are displayed in places such as the Egyptian Museum in Cairo and the British Museum in London.

Ancient Egypt continues to interest people around the world. They visit museums to see ancient objects up close. Tourists visit the pyramids at Giza and the tombs in the Valley of the Kings. They sail along the same Nile River as the ancient Egyptians did. They learn about famous figures, such as King Tut and Cleopatra. They also create books, movies, and plays about ancient Egypt.

Scientists are learning new ways to study mummies and other pieces of history. But many questions remain. People will keep exploring the great mysteries of ancient Egyptian civilization for years to come.

12 Key Dates

2670 BCE
King Djoser makes the first step pyramid.

2613 BCE
The Old Kingdom begins.

2600 BCE
Egyptians begin to purposely
mummify the dead.

2550 BCE
King Khufu builds the Great Pyramid
at Giza.

2055 BCE
The Middle Kingdom begins.

1550 BCE
The New Kingdom begins.

332 BCE
Alexander the Great leads the Macedonians
into Egypt.

30 BCE
Octavian defeats Cleopatra, and Egypt becomes part of the Roman Empire.

394 CE
The last known inscription of hieroglyphs is carved.

1798 CE
Napoleon invades Egypt.

1799 CE
A French soldier discovers the Rosetta Stone.

1922 CE
King Tut's tomb is discovered in the Valley of the Kings.

Glossary

amulet
A small charm or object worn to protect against evil.

archaeologist
A person who studies objects from the past.

arithmetic
Math that deals with adding, subtracting, multiplying, or dividing.

artifact
Something made by humans.

delta
An area where a river splits into smaller rivers before flowing into the ocean.

geometry
Math that deals with angles and lines.

irrigation
A waterway that carries water to crops.

myth
A traditional story of a people.

plateau
A high, flat area of land.

rituals
Events that are repeated in the same way.

silt
Fine sand or rock material left by a river.

Valley of the Kings
A valley on the Nile's west bank; home to many royal tombs.

For More Information

Books

Asselin, Kristine Carlson. *Pharaohs and Dynasties of Ancient Egypt.* Mankato, MN: Capstone Press, 2012.

Boyer, Crispin. *Everything Ancient Egypt.* Washington, DC: National Geographic Kids, 2011.

Kenney, Karen Latchana. T*he Mystery of the Sphinx.* Minneapolis: Abdo, 2016.

Malam, John. *Mummies.* New York: Gareth Stevens, 2015.

Visit 12StoryLibrary.com

Scan the code or use your school's login at **12StoryLibrary.com** for recent updates about this topic and a full digital version of this book. Enjoy free access to:

- Digital ebook
- Breaking news updates
- Live content feeds
- Videos, interactive maps, and graphics
- Additional web resources

Note to educators: Visit 12StoryLibrary.com/register to sign up for free premium website access. Enjoy live content plus a full digital version of every 12-Story Library book you own for every student at your school.

Index

About the Author

Laura K. Murray is the Minnesota-based author of more than 40 nonfiction books for children. She enjoys learning about the fascinating lives of ancient peoples and how they compare with our lives today.